Life after Death

Behind   The   Screen   Door

Gary Smart

outskirts
press

Dedication
This book is dedicated with love to
my deceased mother, Ms. Lucille Smart,
and dad, Willie Smart, Sr., and siblings Willie Smart, Jr.,
Morton Smart, Herbert Smart, Herman Smart
and Dorothy Smart

Table of Contents

Acknowledgments

First and foremost, I would like to thank God, who's the head of my life, for making it all possible.

I would like to thank my deceased parents: my father, Mr. Willie Smart, and my mother, Lucille Carlo Smart, for bringing me into this world with love. I would like to thank my siblings for being a part of my life through the ups and downs. Michelle Smart, Dwight Smart, Benjamin Smart, and my deceased siblings, you are gone but not forgotten, I will always love you all. May God continue to keep you in his care.

I would like to thank God for blessing me with a son by the name of Ladarris Carlo Smart. Daddy loves you and you will always be my pride and joy. And thank you, Lord, for blessing me with grandkids Aaliyah Smart, Ladarris Smart, Jr., and Legend Smart. Papa loves you all. I thank you, Lord, for my nieces and nephews Marquita Smart, Baron, Malcolm, Dwight Smart, Jr., Tawshawna Smart, Shawntia Smart, John Wilson, Lisa Smart, Nicky, Benjamin Smart, Maurice Nelson, and my sister-in-law Gloria Smart.

I really want to give special thanks for my extended family and friend Gregory Cousar Roper, Sr. for his directions on pushing me to get this story out. I also thank my godsister Nicole Trahan, who guided me along the way while writing this story. She put up with a lot of me aggravating her, but through it all it's completed. Special thanks; I love you.

I really thank my co-worker Natividat Ramos, Reginald Carthen for being more than a co-worker, being very supportive, having a great sense of humor, and always having suggestions and ideas.

I would really love to thank Elaine Deering, who did a wonderful job with her editorial skills; she made it all come to reality.

I would like to give shout outs to my cousins and classmates, you know who you are. Thank each and every one of you—I love you. Now you all go out and support me by purchasing a book.

Gary Smart

Introduction

THIS IS THE story of a young kid who lost both of his parents at an early age. How he experienced his father being murdered in front of his own eyes. How it haunts him year after year until he tells his side of the story. How drugs were in his life, and how drugs played a role in one of his sibling's life. How badly his siblings were treated while living with their Auntie Regina.

It was so hard to cope with life and the things that he was experiencing at such a young age. Cameron was torn between life and death. His neighbors cursed his family for some strange reason. He and his siblings were locked up in the room every day until it was time to eat. Living on the streets, he snuck out the window of Regina's house. Now he tried to find himself and figure some things out on his own as he ran from state to state, looking for answers, trying to make a living doing what he could to survive. One day he ran into the right person, who sought help for him and got him back on the right track. This spiritual advisor had a lot to do with the 180 degree turnaround for the best that he made.

CHAPTER 1

Childhood Escapades

MANY YEARS AGO, my family and I lived in an old house with a fireplace located on a dead end street in a pretty small town in Florida called Coconut Grove; the floors squeaked and the back porch was unstable. We were nine kids and two parents living in a small house.

Back then, it was nice quiet place, with only four houses on the block where we lived.

I know my mother and father did a wonderful job taking care of us. I am sure they were not making much money. To have such a big family is a big responsibility; raising kids, making sure they have food on the table and a roof over their heads, and a belief in the sanctity of marriage.

Our neighborhood was pretty friendly and we had a lot of activities going on there. Video games and computers were not as popular as they are now, so we created our own fun. We used to play football every day after school, go cart racing, play basketball, and run track. I can remember when I used to play football in the streets, I always thought I could fly, so I would catch the football when they threw it to me and leap

1

up as if I were Superman to make quite a few touchdowns. We would take a shopping cart and cut the top off to make a race cart out of it. We used to take a sheet, make a parachute out of it, and jump off the roof of our house.

Going to the drag races with my father gave us the idea to race shoes down the hallway of our house. We had this long hallway in our home that was our drag strip. The things we used to race down the hall were shoes, marbles and feathers in the air. We found all kinds of ways of playing together. We also had b-b guns and would go into our back yard and shoot bottles. Coming from a big family, we really did not need any friends. There were enough of us to enjoy one another's company.

There was also a lot of bullying and fighting going on, but we were back to being friends minutes later.

There were times I was pushed to turn around and fight my best friend. We were all best friends, so I did not want to fight. I used to be scared to fight, as the other boys were taller than me. My brother used to say, "If you don't fight back, that's an ass whipping." So I fought my friend. I went to his house, beat him up, and ran all the way home. Later his father came over to our house and asked what happened. I lied and told him his son used to bully me, so we fought and that's what happened. My friend's father said to me he better not catch me over at his house ever again. I was a little sad and happy at the same time. From then on, I went around starting fights, as I had gotten over the fear of fighting.

One day my mother and father had to work, so my dad called my Aunt Regina over to babysit my siblings and me. My brothers Randall and Joseph got bored watching a magician on television, so they decided they would perform their own magic acts. My parents had an old trunk that was used for their important papers. We all thought it would be a good idea to lock my sister in there and see if a trick could make her disappear, unaware of the danger and harm we could have caused her. The lock jammed as we waved the magic wand and nothing helped; she was stuck, panicking, screaming, and crying. We couldn't get her out.

Aunt Regina was cooking while this took place on our front porch. My brothers and I tried everything we could think of, including cutting her out, which led to us cutting ourselves. We prayed and then came up with a new plan that worked, which was to cut a hole big enough to get her out of the trunk. Our mom was just pulling in the driveway shortly after we got her out. We quickly wiped the tears from our sister's eyes and pretended to be playing like normal kids. My mom was clueless; she walked in the door and said, "How's everyone doing? Hope you all did not give Regina a hard time." We were all just hoping our little sister did not tell mother or father what happened; they would have surely beat our ass.

Several days later Regina was asked to babysit us again. This time we played outside with friends, but for some reason, I went in the house. Distracted by a box of matches, I took them up to my room and started playing with them. This was more exciting than playing outside. Aunt Regina was in the living room with my baby sister. All of a sudden, things got out of control; a lit match fell on my bed. Within minutes, a small fire had started on my bed, so I tried to put out the fire with a cup of water from the kitchen. When I returned to my room, the fire had spread from my bed to the room, and then our entire home burned up in flames.

At first, I ran out of the house without telling my aunt. This one of the worst days of my life; I was scared. My aunt eventually grabbed my sister Ebony and ran out the door. I ran across the street to our neighbors' home. When Betty came to the door, I told her, "There's a fire at my house." This was devastating; the neighbors watched as our home burned to the ground. We lost everything; furniture and clothes all gone. What a tragedy!

Aunt Regina called my parents while the firefighters assisted. They came home to nothing. When my parents arrived, they asked if everyone was okay and then wanted to know what happened. I dropped my head, embarrassed and scared. I did not know what was going to happen to me. When the fire chief questioned me, I told the truth, that I was playing with matches and the bed caught on fire. While crying, I kept saying, "I'm sorry." My family and I moved into temporary housing until our new home was built.

Because of this incident, I received counseling a few days a week. I watched films about the dangers of playing with fire; I learned that many people did not survive fires.

As the years passed, my siblings and I used to play football in the streets against another street in our neighborhood. When either team won or lost, we would fight against the winning team; no one wanted to be a loser. Also, during the 4th of July holiday, our block had a competition against another block. The only thing I can remember is the time Randall's arm was on fire, but as the days passed, we all became friends again.

At some point disobeying and stealing started becoming a part of my life, which is not a good thing. I really think that what led me to start stealing from stores was that when I was a child I didn't know any better, but I felt I held on to that excuse too long. I remember as a child going into a store for a bag of cookies, just sitting in the store eating them while my father was shopping. The salesman never said anything to me as if they were free. I guess I had that hungry look on my face, and besides, it was too late, the bag of cookies was almost gone.

On the weekends, we used to watch cartoons on Saturday morning, when all of my favorite cartoons are on TV. I would be glued to our television set, sitting close, having a big bowl of cereal and milk. One day, my cousin stopped by our house to watch TV with us. After a few moments he got up and changed the channel because he did not like the cartoons we were watching. I was about 7 years old at the time. I politely asked him to turn the channel back, and he pushed me. Before I knew it, I picked up a bottle and hit him in the head with it, and blood spurted everywhere.

I ran out the door, ran for a mile and a half to where my father was working, all out of breath. Finally I reached my dad and told him what happened. My dad brought my cousin and me back home and told my cousin he had to go home, that he was wrong, and he was not allowed over any more. My brothers did not know what happened until my dad brought me back home. I must say I was a spoiled kid. My dad would beat me if I was in the wrong, and he might fuss at me, but he would always protect me if he thought I was right.

Being the baby boy of a family of 9 siblings was a plus in some circumstances. I can remember when the holidays approached, a special day would happen, and my father would purchase me whatever I wanted, such as new shoes, suits, and slacks. I never wore old clothes when the holidays came around. I refused to wear hand-me-down clothes. Right then I knew I was going to be a problem child.

I can also remember when my family, cousins and friends would get together for a family gathering. At the gathering, we would have soul food, games, and soul train line dancing. The families competed for money; it was a contest, a battle of the families. I had a cousin who they called Weenie, the same cousin who I once cracked in the head with a bottle. He and I had a battle like when Michael Jackson and James Brown did the dance called The Split. I used to jump up in the air and land in a split position, splitting my pants as well, laughing. I had my Afro and my pointed shoes which could smash a roach in a corner. I won the contest for a modest prize, but $5 back then that was a lot of money for a kid. Ever since, I was hustling, as a dancer making money, at family gatherings. We also had awesome Easter egg hunts on Easter. It was wonderful how we connected with one another and became one big family.

These gatherings made me realize how important it is get close and spend your time enjoying another. It's bad when you have siblings and you don't communicate with them as you should, never sit and talk, showing love toward one another. I had a brother who I really did not know like I should have or wanted to. He was hardly ever home, always in the streets; he was dating a young lady and moved in with her. As the years passed, I got a little older; he and his girl were spending a lot of time together. Years passed by and I heard he was ill. I moved away for a minute and once I returned, I found out that he had passed away. I did not get a chance to see him; it really broke my heart. I was upset with myself, because I should have pushed to communicate with him. The sad thing was his son was ill as well; I heard his son had died months before my brother.

The lesson that I got out of the tragedy that my brother experienced was that each day and any time you can, call your siblings, parents, sons, daughters, grandchildren, etc. and tell them how much you love them. Spend quality time trying to do what's right on this earth; remember, the Lord granted you this time. Throughout the years, I have had so many brothers pass away a few years apart, at a young age. I could never understand that. I know that we all have our time here on this earth; it was like a curse on my family--the deaths of my siblings were at least 3 years apart.

Imagine growing up and never getting as close to your family as you would like. I always wanted to have that brother-to-brother talk with my older brother who is next to the oldest. I would have hung out with them or shared certain activities, not knowing that they were not going to be around as long in my life to watch me grow older. I'm not questioning the work of the Lord; He has his reasons why He does what He does. He never makes mistakes. I know how precious time is now, so we need to embrace each other and express what we want to while we have breath in our bodies. I really miss my siblings, but have not forgotten them; they were just gone too soon.

CHAPTER 2

Neighborhood Shenanigans

ALTHOUGH OUR FAMILY was so large we always had plenty of playmates, we also got to know our neighbors over the years. We had a nosy neighbor who lived across the street. The lady was very wicked; she never liked people standing in front of her house. My friends and I used to sit outside near her house all night just talking about school, etc., so she would come outside and try to run us off. We would call her all kinds of names such as mean wicked witch, as she never cared for company. Well, at least not our company.

Once the old lady caught us, she had a tight death grip; it was hard to get away from her. She also had a broomstick she would try to beat us with; she used that same broom to sweep her driveway and her garden. She had a yard that looked like a scary forest, especially on Halloween. As the years passed, we had not seen her for some days, only to find out later that she had died. We were kind of sad; we missed her, as wicked as she was.

At home playing in our backyard, we had these other neighbors who did not like us. They were an older couple with no kids, just pets. One day I overheard them saying they were going to put a curse on everyone in our household. That really shook me up. As time progressed, I never forgot about what I had overheard. I never discussed that with anyone, but still thought about it from time to time. I always kept it at the back of my mind and paid close attention to my family members, thinking maybe that had something to do with my mother's death.

Another neighbor who lived next door to us when I was a kid had a couple of older people living with her and a house full of kittens and dogs. Some of her grandkids lived there also. Every day when I would come home from school, I would stop by and visit her, always trying to hustle and make a dollar or two. At that time I was attending elementary school. After I reached home and finished my homework and chores around the house, I would go over to my neighbor's house. She would have me doing some side jobs for her, such as going to the store, mowing her lawn, or mopping her patio floor. Her house used to stink so badly; she was an older lady who could not hold her bladder, so it would smell like animals and urine.

My neighbor had an older gentleman living with her; he had to be about 70 years old. I used to pick on this guy who had back issues that caused posture problems. He would sit in a rocking chair with his cane. My friends and I would try to take his cane from him and run, knowing he could not move as fast as we could. One day he grabbed us with a tight death grip and started pounding us with his cane, laughing. It took two people to unlock this man's fingers from around our hands; he was just that strong. I started feeling bad for what I had done. I had to pray and ask the Lord to forgive us for picking on this man for no reason. I guess we were just being disrespectful kids at the time.

It was so bad, this older man would come to me in my sleep. I had nightmares about him because I knew what I did was wrong and it was on my conscience. I always respected my elders; I did not know where that lapse came from. Disrespecting your parents or your elders is not a good feeling at all. One day, if we live long enough, we would not like that to happen to us, so I told my friends the next day that we were going over to the neighbor's house next door and apologize to this elderly guy because what we did was not nice. So as we approached the guy the very next day, he reached for his cane. I said, "Sir, we just want to apologize to you. We never meant you any harm. We were just being stupid, disrespectful kids." So we talked to him and laughed with him.

As the weeks passed, we had not seen this guy sitting outside in the yard in his rocking chair for some time, so I asked the lady whose house it was what happened to the older guy. She replied, "Oh, he died a couple of days ago." My heart felt so heavy. I really felt bad, but I said to myself at least my friends and I got a chance to apologize to this elderly man. So I saved up enough money to purchase a card for the older guy and asked my neighbor to please put it in his casket for me. Two weeks later, the older lady died also.

It was a gloomy day, but I thank GOD for my being so nice to her, helping her around the house, and apologizing to the gentleman. The only people left in the lady's house were the grandkids and their father, and a house full of kittens and dogs. So I went over and did one final cleaning. As I was cleaning up the house, the father of the grandkids said his mom had left me some money to clean for the next 2 weeks. It was so strange because she was no longer there. The moral of this story is please be respectful to your parents and elders; you do not know when it will be the last time you communicate with someone who means so much to you.

CHAPTER 3

School Days

SCHOOL DAYS ARE supposed to be one of the happiest times of your life, although at the time, it seems like a lot of work keeping you from having fun. Nevertheless, we had our fun times as well. We walked to school every day. We had a great time at that school; it had a tennis court, basketball court, and swings.

One day I was getting ready for school and noticed we were out of lotion. My parents always told us to lotion up, brush our hair, etc., so I took it upon myself to put quantities of grease on my legs, hoping they would not be ashy. I had so much grease on my legs while playing on the playground in the dirt, I would fall and my legs would be covered with sand, grass, etc. because these things stuck to grease. I was so embarrassed.

While attending elementary school, my brother and I used to run track and we were the fastest runners there during track and field day. I also played tennis and practiced every day, not knowing a TV production team was coming to film me. Yes, I was on TV playing tennis representing my school, which inspired me to do something in life.

I also have fond memories of walking home from school. There was a school bus that would pick us up in the morning to take us to school, but I chose to walk home from school with my friends. Walking 7 miles from school was fun; I looked forward to that. We would do a lot of things you weren't supposed to do such as getting in fights, stopping by friends' houses, stopping by the store to play video games, stealing from the stores, taking whatever we wanted and running, and stopping by the park to play a few games.

There were days my little sister Ebony would walk home from school with us. We used to have a police officer patrolling the school area on a horse riding up and down the street. One day as school was letting out, we were walking home talking about what happened in class. Ebony was talking and not looking where she was going. She walked smack into a stop sign, her eyebrow started bleeding, and my little sister started crying. The police officer was passing by at the time and called out, "I seen you hit her." He called other police officers over until my sister finally stopped crying, and told them she ran into the sign without looking. Once we got home, we bandaged her up.

Sometimes on our way home from school, my brothers and I would fight our friends. We would kick the back of their shoes, making them trip over themselves. One day, as my brother and I were walking to the store next to the school, I guess I met my match when this kid came up to us and asked for our money. My brother Randall said "No" and I was scared. The guy pulled out a knife and started coming toward us. Randall stopped and said, "I'm not running," so my brother started fighting the guy while I ran away like a coward, leaving Randall to fight alone. My brother knocked the dude down to the ground, and we both ran after that. He threw the knife at us, but it missed us, and so we got away. From then on, I had to brush up on my fighting skills.

In the classroom, I noticed that the teacher needed a pet to tell her everything that was going on in class when he or she was away. A friend and I were that pet, but after school, when the bell rang, the person we snitched on would be waiting for us outside at the park, so we would take the opposite route home. The next day, we would face them head on and quickly got out of that teacher snitching after that issue.

As the years passed, I learned that hanging around the wrong group of friends would get me caught up in something that I have no clear recollection of. I remember this guy was a good friend of mine; we used to walk to school every day, but for some strange reason, something happened in class. I cannot remember what it was we fought over in school, but the teachers had to break us up. After school, we continued that fight as it was not over yet until I got the best of him. I believe he tried to bully me just because I was church going and quiet. I had to let him know that just because I attend church does not mean I'm a pushover. I jumped up behind this dude and choked him until he about passed out. I was a raging bull; I was sick and tired of him trying to bully me.

Well, I never had any problems out of him again.

Our parents taught us that if someone hit us, we better fight back or that meant an ass whooping once we get home. If they are bigger than we are, they told us to pick up something and knock the "crap" out of them and run. After that, they will not bother us again; they would think that we were crazy.

When report card time came, we had a favorite uncle who would come by our home on report card day to see who had a good report card so he could reward us. As a kid, our teacher would give us smiling faces or stars or some kind of sticker for recognizing that we were doing great in school, and our favorite uncle would give us 5 dollars for each smiling face or star or an A on our report card. This was a great incentive that made me want to do my best, not just for the money, but to make my parents and my uncle proud.

CHAPTER 4

A Mother's Love Is Forever

AFTER THE FIRE that burned down my childhood home, we were all excited to move into our new home. My parents were happy also, but just when things were starting to look up, tragedy hit again. One day my mom was rushed to the hospital and she was admitted. We'd visit her after school until she was released from the hospital. She seemed so happy when she returned home, but the doctor told her to take it easy and get plenty of rest. Her heart wasn't very strong. Hospitals were not as advanced as they are today, and they could not offer her any options.

One Wednesday morning, I woke up and got ready for school. I went to give my mother a kiss on the lips and a hug; I told her I loved her and was glad she was home. Off to school my brothers and I went. When I came home from school, my mom was not feeling well. I began massaging and rubbing lotion on her legs, something I'd do every day after school. In fact, these were some of my happiest memories.

My mother was normally on her feet all day; she worked for one of the Kennedys as a maid. Friday evening, that same week, on my way home from school, my siblings and

I noticed the police and rescue wagon at our house. We ran home, wondering what was going on. Just before walking into our house, my dad met us and said mom had died. All of a sudden, something came over me; I could not move, talk, scream, or cry. She slipped away from me without my saying again, "I love you." No more massaging her feet or ankles. It was a very bad day, very blue for my siblings and me; my dad was sad and heartbroken. I guess God had better plans for her; he did not want her to suffer any more. He knew she was weak; her heart could take no more pain.

I can remember when I was 6 years old, and mumbled a terrible word under my breath because I couldn't have my way on something. I am so ashamed at the memory, I don't want to repeat it. I was devastated when my mother slipped away from me, knowing she was the best mother a child could ever have. All that time not knowing my mother had a bad heart, I felt a little responsible for some of the pain she felt.

One day when my mother was driving through the neighborhood, as I was walking behind the car, she accidentally hit me with the bumper of her car, not knowing I was behind her and not at first realizing what had happened. She got out of the car running and screaming, asking, "are you okay?" I replied, "Yes, mother."

I have been holding on to that memory forever. I will never let that memory go; it brings tears of joy to my eyes. We must appreciate our parents and show them how much we love them and thank GOD for them. You never know when they're not coming back. And all these years, I still wish my mother Happy Mothers Day.

CHAPTER **5**

Father's Days

MY FATHER WAS a hard working man who believed in taking care of his family. He was a contractor; he built homes and also worked as a mechanic. He also built cars to drag race on the weekend; I enjoyed going to the racetrack with him. The races often took place in Hollywood, Florida. What I enjoyed the most was riding with him as a passenger while he drag raced against his competitors and won trophies and money.

Spending time with my dad meant a lot to me. I can re-member the times my father and I used to go fishing; I went with him a couple of times. We would pack our lunch and leave about 5 a.m. to fish; that's the time the fish bite and are hungry. We would have sardines, meat loaf, and crackers; it was nice. He tried to teach me how to fish, putting the bait on the fishing pole. I would swing the pole out into the water and end up hooking his cigarettes out of his shirt pocket. How funny that was; I had a great time! We caught mullets, catfish, snappers, and even an eel; we had to throw him back. The only bad thing was we had mosquitoes and flies out annoying us at that time of morning.

One day my father took my brother and me to work with him. My dad worked as a mechanic part-time for the gas station, so my brother and I sat in the car waiting for him to get off work. Dad asked us to get out and help pump the customers' gas and clean their windows, as it was a full service gas station, so my brother and I did what normal young kids do, started playing, which turned into a fight. We were fighting over the tips which we received from the customers, so I jumped on top of my dad's car. I was lying on the roof of the car when my brother came behind me and pushed me off the car. I fell face down and started crying like never before. My dad came running out of the shop. I had a bruise from the top of my forehead to the bottom of my chin, so next day I went to school looking like a bandaged patient.

I deserved that; I'm always doing something to piss my brothers off, as I'm the baby boy. This tells you how spoiled I was. I can recall one day my dad was getting his car ready for the drag race for the weekend. As he worked on his car, I was standing outside pouting because I wanted to go to my grandmother's house. My dad said we'd go once he finished working on his car. My big mama always had sweets and junk food for us, and I guess I had a sweet tooth at the time, so I told my dad, "I can't wait, I want to go now." He said "no," so I whispered something out of my mouth and ran out. By the time I reached the door, he threw me his glue can that he used to seal head gaskets on the car. I was just about to step into the house, when the can hit me in the lip and cut my lip. Blood was all over the door.

After this incident, I never mumbled or whispered anything to him again. I have that same cut under my lip today. My brothers were feeling sorry for me, but that was due to me and my "slick" mouth.

As the years passed, my father started dating again; with his being a single parent after my mom was deceased, I tried to understand what my father was feeling after my mother passed away and was no longer here on earth anymore. I wondered how he felt about raising 9 children on his own. There were times I would catch him staring out the window in deep thought. As the years passed, I could see my dad was starting to get back to normal. He was smiling and laughing again, but watching my dad dating was a tough pill to swallow. He's human, I respect that. Although the years passed, my mom's death was still fresh in my mind.

Coincidentally, my dad started speaking to our neighbor who lived across the street from us. As the days went by, he kept getting a lot closer to this lady across the street. Whenever the neighbor stopped by, he'd introduce us to her. She was a very nice person and single at the time. This neighbor would invite my dad to go fishing with her, and so in the early morning, they would go fishing together.

My dad really liked this lady. We would talk to her from time to time. There were times she would spend the night at our house. As we got to know her, we would talk with her to see what she was really like. She invited us to her daughter's house, who lived in another city about 30 minutes from where we lived. So we would go over and eat dinner at her daughter's house and spend the weekend. We would play with her daughter's kids and as the years passed, we became close like family. Although my dad's relationship with the young lady did not last, we stayed close to the family. Betty, the daughter of my dad's girlfriend, became my brother Randall's godmother, so we would go over to their house for holidays, birthday parties, and Easter.

LIFE AFTER DEATH: BEHIND THE SCREEN DOOR

A few years later, my father was dating again and this time was thinking about getting married. I noticed my dad was speaking to the young lady who moved next door to us with her two kids. She was a smoker and she drank, which concerned me. My dad did not drink, so I thought that she was not good enough for him, but as time passed, they grew close and started talking about getting married. That was a tough pill to swallow. I knew my father must have a life, but it was just a little puzzling to me. My mom was not around anymore and I had to accept that my dad was human.

So years passed, my dad was remarried to this young lady, and things were going pretty well. I finally got used to her being around and in the same house with us. So now I had a stepmom. That was kind of strange; I never expected that. We got along pretty well with her as long as she stayed in her lane.

As the months passed, things got a little crazy. There were some nights I used to hear them arguing, which kept me up. I was not used to that; my mom and dad got along pretty well, so this was something we had to get used to just because my dad married her and loved her. As the days passed, it got a little better.

My stepmom used to bring her kids over so we could play together and become one family, but I just could not swallow that. It took plenty of time for me to adjust to that, but as time allows, we were getting close and I had to respect her just because she was my dad's new wife. We used to sit up and talk like one big family.

Everything was going great until she started to drink. I can remember one day as I was entering the kitchen, she and my dad were there talking. She got loud and started fighting. I jumped in the middle, trying to stop the fight while my

20

siblings were in the other room watching TV. She pushed me away while they were fighting, so I jumped up and before you knew it, I was behind her, kicking her in the ass several times. I was only 7 years old at the time, but I loved my dad so much, I was always there by his side, no matter what was going on. My mom was no longer here; I had my dad to protect. Then I was crying because my mom and dad never fought as far as I can remember. I missed my mom so much; she never drank or smoked. Now my dad was dealing with this drinker and smoker.

After that I mentally told myself that my mom was his real wife, that this woman was not worthy to be married to him. I reminded myself that my stepmom was so intoxicated she probably had no idea what she was doing, and I wished my father would just leave her, but I know he was brought up to believe in the sanctity of marriage, and only death would cause them to part.

Eventually they separated and we never heard from her again. Three years later, my brother read in the paper that she had died. Thus ended a marriage that in many ways I wished had never happened in the first place.

CHAPTER **6**

I Let God into My Life

AS THE YEARS passed by, I started attending church more often. There were days we had Youth Day at the church and the pastor would love for me to sing. I was a deacon at church there and would deliver the young deacon's message and pray on that day. In order to present the message, you must study your Bible and be ready to deliver it on Sunday. I would read my message that the Lord gave me and explain it. I really enjoyed that; right then I knew I was a special person.

God also prepared messages for me to take to school and enlighten others. I would take my Bible to school and read it on my break and explain it to others. My classmates would tease me and call me names such as "little church boy" and "nerdy kid," which did not bother me, because I knew I was doing what the Lord wanted me to do, and I did not want to lose who I really was.

After dad remarried and was involved in constant fights with his new wife, I started attending church every Sunday as well as Tuesday and Thursday nights. There were times I would go to church and come home and read my Bible for 30 minutes. I would pray for my family every day and ask the

Lord to look over my dad. Ever since he married this lady, there were issues. I used to sit up and talk to the good Lord; He would grace me with wisdom and knowledge. I would read about how He healed the sick and raised the dead, how He's always there when you need Him and He's your protector.

Attending church more often was a good thing to do on a Thursday night. While in church, we had a special prayer service for anyone who needed special prayer—As young as I was, I did not know how that really worked, but as the preacher was preaching, I was mesmerized. Once when I was standing in line for prayer, all of a sudden I felt a push as if someone touched me or pushed me. As I turned around, no one was there, so I laughed. Right then I said to myself, "I guess that was the spirit of the Lord and God is real." Ever since then, I was a believer.

Every Tuesday and Thursday night and Sunday morning, I was there in church waiting for the service to begin and for pastor Cheryl Williams to preach. As I attended the church and was feeling the spirit of the Lord, I was baptized and saved. I was promoted to be a young deacon in the church. I joined the usher board and became a member of the choir. Later I started playing the drums in church. Ever since then, I felt the presence of the Lord and that was the best feeling ever, so I would read the Bible a lot and pray and talk to the Lord. He's our father. I would talk to Him throughout the day, knowing He was always there as a protector and an advisor who never guides me wrong. The devil tried to interfere several times, but my mind always stayed on the Lord. I loved the Spirit I was feeling, knowing it was right and a powerful feeling. Amen.

I would attend Bible study and prayer sessions a lot to stay closer to my Father. As the years passed, I was getting a few years older and getting closer to the Lord. One Sunday night, I had a wonderful time in church; the message was strong. That Sunday night, once I reached home, I took my shoes off. As I was lying down on the couch where my dad was sleeping, I could not sleep. My heart was racing. I could not understand what was going on with me, so I would sit up for a minute, and then my heart would slow down. I would try to lie down again, but once I laid down, my heart would start racing again. So I would sit up, get my Bible, and begin to read several verses of the Bible. After reading my Bible, I would doze off to sleep.

As I was sleeping, the Lord was talking to me; he showed me a vision in which I witnessed my father's death. My little brother got into an argument with this older guy, so I told my dad about it. My dad and I drove over to this guy's house, which was about a half a mile from where we lived. As we reached the guy's home, my dad got out of the car. He told me to stay in the car, that he would be right back. As I sat in the car, my father knocked on the guy's screen door. He answered and I could hear them talking. Then I heard them arguing (remember I was just 10 years old at this time). A few minutes later I heard a gunshot, which came from behind the screen door. As I was slowly getting out of the car, I saw my father stumbling downstairs and drop down to the ground. I screamed and cried as I ran over to him shouting, "Dad, get up!" as he took his last breath, telling me he loved me. That was my vision; the Lord was preparing me for the future.

As the days passed, I never told anyone about that vision. Days later that vision came true the exact way the Lord showed me. He had already prepared me. I could not cry and there was nothing I could do to prevent that from happening. God has His reasons and I would never question Him. I continued attending church, which helped me cope with a lot of situations that I was experiencing as a child. God continued showing me things that I could not prevent from happening.

After that, I became a junior deacon in the church, and the church nominated me to attend a church seminar and represent our church. That meant attending the headquarters church in Nashville, Tennessee, which oversaw all the other churches. My job was to attend these seminars, take notes, and turn in a report on the discussions of the church, which I was graded on. I took good notes and at the end of the week, we would receive grades on our notes and a quiz presenting reports to our church. Of course I received an A or B on my activities, never anything less.

As the years passed, I was feeling a lot more involved and not missing my parents as much. In church I was taught that GOD is your father and mother. I feel that if you have a close bond with the Lord, anything you are going through too shall pass. My parents are gone but not forgotten. My encouraging words to you who are going through something troubling is that you have to go through the good and the bad and the rough times to appreciate the sunshine; there has to be rain in your life to appreciate the sunshine at the end of the deluge.

CHAPTER **7**

The Reign of Regina and Godmother Betty

A FEW MONTHS after my father's death, my dad's sister Regina had custody of my younger siblings and me. You know the saying, as sad as it sounds, no one would treat you like your parents. Years passed living with my auntie, knowing she was only there for the money which was left behind from my dad's social security. She was a money hungry bitch and very evil. She was bitter the whole time we were under her care. Her main concern was collecting money. She never gave us anything. She never allowed us to go outside and mingle with the other kids; if we did, that was a problem, so we would just sit in the house all day.

One day a tragedy struck in the house as my little sister lay sleeping on the chair in the living room, while Regina was in the kitchen cooking. In the kitchen was a back door. As Regina poured out hot grease, instead of using the back door, she would come through the living room where my sister was sleeping on the chair. On one of these trips she spilled white hot cooking grease in my sister's lap, which scorched her and left 3rd degree burns on her leg. My sister had to stay in the hospital for months, receiving all kinds of skin grafts. Thank God that He healed her from the burns and mental issues throughout that tragedy.

My escape from Regina's home was attending church on Tuesday and Thursday nights and on Sunday mornings. Those days were the best time of my life. There were times Regina would try to stop me from attending church. I would escape out of the bedroom window to attend church and deal with whatever situation faced me when I returned home. Whenever I wanted to go outside to play with my friends, I would lock the bedroom door as if I were in there asleep and jump out the window. I would return later through the window; it was just that bad back then. I would pray and talk to the Lord, trying to find a way out of my auntie's house for my siblings and me. Oh, how I really missed my parents!

I knew once my parents were deceased, I didn't have that mother or father figure in my life around anymore, but the pastor at my church took plenty of time out of her busy schedule to have one-on-one Bible study with me at her house, and traveling with her, she played a big role in my life. There were days we would have prayer. I would request special prayers for my family, my siblings. After church, my pastor would take my siblings out to eat dinner with her and her kids, and if any kind of church event would come up, she would take us shopping and buy clothes. All of these positive things would inspire me to do better in life and stay focused in church and in school. She helped me to understand the death of my parents and how to move on in life and read scriptures out of the Bible.

It was so ironic that the church I attended was my cousin's auntie's church, because her auntie's brother was my cousin.

She would treat me as if I were her child. I joined the church; I felt the Lord sent me to her. I sometimes felt my mother caring for me through her. Attending church really helped me cope with a lot of situations that I was experiencing, and how GOD showed me things that I could not prevent from happening.

I admit there were times I was a disobedient kid, stealing from stores, being rude to adults and being disrespectful to my elders, hurting people who tried to help me. I used to act out on my mother, who did not deserve any of it. There was a time when drugs took over my brother's life for some years. My brother was a very bright young man throughout his years in school; he was one of the top of the class, with beautiful kids. After his wife died, he turned to the streets and went from drugs to all kind of drugs.

Here I was, a young man who had so much to deal with at a young age. I knew I couldn't fix everyone's problems. During church service one night, I asked for prayers for my family. During the time of my dad's death, I learned always to tell my parents how much I loved them. There were times I was angry with my parents, just because I could not have things my way. I would mumble to myself how I wished my mother would die, not meaning it, but I was angry at the time, not knowing how it would affect my life. I really miss her and I apologize today as many times as I can.

As the years passed and dad died, we stayed in touch with my siblings' godmother. As we became teenagers, we asked, "Can we live with you?" She opened her arms and welcomed us into her home. She took us in as if we were her kids. Betty never treated us different from her own kids. She would buy this red fruit punch that she called "jungle juice." We drank tons of jungle juice and ate lots of bologna sandwiches, but we still enjoyed it. Today, years later, we are still connected as one big family. You never forget the good and bad times.

My brother's godmother also helped me get a job at the same place where she was employed. I used to work in a warehouse, which was a pretty good job. I had the best time working there; it was like a workout. The people there were so friendly, the pay was pretty good, and I was fresh out of school. She provided a ride to work for me and I would catch a ride home, so I tried not to ask for much, but the one thing that was funny, Betty never really liked to say no to me. I used to ask her if I could use her car to hang out. She would not answer, then she would come back to me later, take a deep breath and say, "Go ahead." After she did all that, I would change my mind sometimes, and laugh.

Regardless, Betty was a great godmother, and a good mother figure. I must say she really maintained a lot of her parental duties. She was a single parent, and always provided the best for her kids and godkids. When Thanksgiving came around, she would make all kinds of food, desserts, etc. I remember her making an awesome potato salad. As we were sitting around the table while dinner was being prepared, the back glass sliding door was open, and a fly got into the house. He wanted to buzz around the food, so as he flew low, I took a piece of paper, took a swing at him, and turned the whole potato salad bowl over. There went the best side dish, but we had a wonderful Thanksgiving. It was just like one big happy family.

As I was getting ready to graduate from high school, depression really struck me. It was a sad day for me; my mother and father were deceased and my older sibling was on drugs. As I walked across that stage, there was no one there to congratulate me for the effort I put forth to graduate from high school. I shouted out my name saying, "Great job, Cameron.

We are proud of you." Then I felt the presence in the stadium from heaven, as though they were looking over me, which brought tears to my eyes, letting me know it's okay.

Then the realization struck me that there was no aunt and no godmother to fall back on; I was on my own, and how I turned out was up to me.

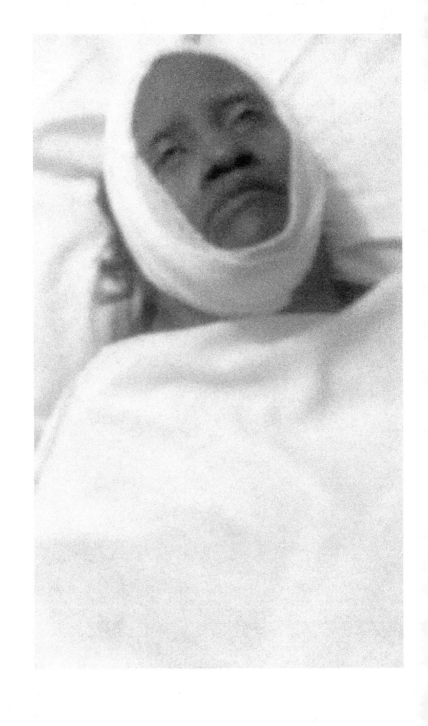

CHAPTER 8

My Special Older Sister

I HAVE AN older sister who was born mentally challenged, with Down Syndrome. She could not speak as clearly as you and I, nor could she understand things like any other normal child. She was attending a special school on a bus that would pick her up for school every morning, where they would try to teach her how to speak and read and interact with others.

As the years passed, she was not progressing as fast as others, but she did understand certain things. I always pray to the Lord that he would one day heal her. Her heart is as strong as that of anyone I have ever known. The funny thing is she would know when you were not feeling well. She would give you a hug and a kiss and a pat on your back, letting you know it was going to be okay. Right then I knew she was touched by the Lord.

Unfortunately, after mom and dad died, and we went to live with Aunt Regina, she treated my sibling with special needs very badly. There were times when Regina would hit my sister on the back of her neck with a shoe, just because she does not understand things clearly like normal people because of her condition. Regina would also call her names, such as dummy. I really had to pray about a lot about the evil things that were happening.

Over the years, my younger sister took the lead in taking care of our special needs sister. At one point my younger sister asked me to move in with her to help me out financially and to assist in the care of my handicapped older sister. And my sister had her own family as well: 3 boys and 1 girl. That was a fresh start for me; I worked helping my sister with bills, and being more responsible. My younger sister and I had a talk about responsibilities, which was a great uplifting conversation that got me on the right track.

While living there, my older sister was not getting any better. We had to wait on her hand and foot, which was not a problem, but her situation was getting a lot worse. She needed 24-hour-a-day assistance, and with both of us working, the kids could only do so much. The doctors said she was not going to live to be over 30 years old, because she's mentally challenged and that's the average life span of a Down syndrome child. But we learned there is no limit with an outpouring of love from GOD and family. We located a facility that takes care of those kinds of patients, enrolled her into the facility, and they are doing a great job with her.

We would go visit our sister every Sunday to make sure she was being treated fairly. Although we were convinced she was in the right place, her condition continued to go downhill. They would rush her to the hospital just about every 3 weeks for things they could not handle. As you can see, my sister required special attention. Then the hospital return visits increased to just about every week, and at the same time, they asked if we would like to put her in hospice. My little sister and I replied, "No."

We know that's a place you go when it comes down to the final days. We still have faith in the Lord, so we would pray every day. We would go by her bedside and ask the good Lord, "What do you want us to do?" We know that it would not be over for her until GOD says it's over. A couple of days later, the doctor called and said she was doing a lot better. He was surprised. We looked at each other and said, "Nothing but Jesus." The hospital and doctors gave up on her a long time ago. They are amazed that she's lived this long, so heed these words of encouragement to you who are experiencing sickness.

My sister at this writing is alive and well, and I know God has a special place in heaven for her.

CHAPTER **9**

I Enter the Working World

SEEING HOW HARD my parents worked to support our family made me realize that the key to prosperity was working. I landed my first job while in the 4th grade, working at a gas station as a service attendant. The gas station was located across the street from the school. My duties were checking oil and pumping gas in the cars and washing windows. I would work at the gas station for 2 hours a day after school. While working there, a production company that was doing a documentary on school kids came and filmed me there, so I was a local celebrity.

I worked at the gas station for about a year, and when that job ended, I landed another job at the five and dime store, watching for people who were trying to steal from the store.

Next, I found a job at the neighborhood grocery store, bagging and helping people with their groceries. "Cameron, come to the front of the store, customers are waiting." I can still hear Mr. Jones' voice yelling at me. Back then I really thought I was making plenty of money when in actuality I was paid only a few dollars. The money used to burn a hole in my pocket, always gone too soon. I would spend it back in the store on junk food, but most of all on toys. If I did not have enough for what I wanted, I'd stand in front of the store and beg strangers for money until I got up enough money to buy what I wanted.

My father's generosity at Christmas time gave me a taste for the finer things in life, so in order to continue my desired lifestyle, I had to continue working and also become a young entrepreneur. As October arrived, I knew that I would be going trick or treating on Halloween with my older brothers. We would go from house to house, getting all kinds of sweets and sometimes money, and I hit upon a scheme to turn this ritual into an opportunity to make money. The very next day after Halloween, I would load my candy into a toy jeep I got for Christmas. I would tie a shoe string to the jeep, start pulling it, and go from house to house on my block, selling candy and bubble gum. The funniest thing, people used to buy things from me; that's how I made extra money to get things I wanted to buy.

When those funds ran out, I was a paperboy, putting packages of papers together and throwing them. I had a bike with a little basket on it, just big enough to hold my papers. I delivered papers on the weekends; I was determined to make some money. I didn't mind going to work to earn spending money.

This strong work ethic has stayed with me throughout my adult life, and I am grateful to my folks for instilling it in me.

CHAPTER **10**

Let the Good Times Roll

LIFE FOR ME was not all work and no play. I put equal effort into enjoying myself. As a teenager, there were plenty of things we could do to stay fit. In addition to tennis, football, and running, we used to stop by the pool, but I could not swim at all. I used to stay in the 3-feet end of the pool, making sure I stayed above the water. My brothers, on the other hand, were good swimmers. I always wanted to learn how to swim, and I've taken swimming lessons but still could not get it together.

I remember my first time learning how to swim. It's so funny; how can you learn how to swim under water rather than on top? I guess one of my fear of drowning was that I would just sink to the bottom. Well, there I was, on top of the water, just paddling my little feet, not really moving anywhere, just making a big splash. As my friends and brothers were laughing at me, I realized I must take my time and get this together, so I started dog paddling, which is a pretty good way to save yourself if you feel you are drowning. I wanted to train myself to swim properly so I wouldn't embarrass myself in front of my friends, so a few days later, I went to the park pool with my brothers. As I sat around the pool, someone out of nowhere threw me into the pool. My heart started racing. I was screaming and crying because I knew I was not a good swimmer. As I came up from the bottom of the pool, I began dog paddling to where I could stand up in the pool. From there, I tried to swim underwater, which was successful for me. Ever since then, I would swim underwater from one side of the pool to the other.

This experience taught me that no matter what situation you get yourself into, if you really want to, you can get yourself out of it. You can succeed--just believe in yourself.

I can remember when I was a kid, there were all kinds of things I wanted to do but was not old enough to do. I couldn't wait to become a teenager, so that I could go plenty of places and do a lot of things, whether good or bad. I used to watch my older brother getting ready to go out clubbing or to parties. I always said to myself that when I got older, I was going to hang out like my brother, not realizing being a kid was even better. You have no bills and no responsibilities except getting up for school, making good grades, and doing a few chores around the house. So as the years pass, you get older and responsibility comes; plenty of homework, time to get a job, and take care of yourself and your own issues.

Now they are drafting teenagers into the army, navy, air force, and marines. All I can think about is people going away and never returning. After becoming a teenager, I changed my way of thinking. I wished I was a kid again; fewer headaches and difficult situations to be put into.

Still, I did get a chance to enjoy the party scene. During the 1970's, we used to go to house parties. Our parents would drop me and my cousin or friends off and come back a couple of hours later to pick us up. There were no fights and no guns at the parties. Everyone there was just enjoying themselves. Those were the days.

Then for a real thrill, there was learning how to drive. I actually started at a young age. I had a brother who was next to my older brother and was in the service for years. Whenever he came home to visit, it was time for me and my brothers to learn how to drive. He drove a 1976 Beetle, 5-speed, light blue. Once our brother entered the house, he would talk to our dad and then take a nap.

While my brother was asleep, we would take his keys off the dresser, open the car door, put the car in neutral, and push it to the end of the block away from the house, so they wouldn't hear us starting up the car. Once we got the car started, we would have to figure out the gear system as we scraped the gears and burned out the clutch. I was 7 years old at that time. My brothers were a few years older than I. We would joyride for an hour. The car would jerk down the streets and cut off. Once the joyride was over, we would pull up on our street, turn the car off, and push it back to the same spot, run in the house, and put the keys back on the dresser.

When my brother woke up, he went to play golf with a few friends. As he entered the car and started the car up, it jerked, as we did not put the car back into neutral when we left the car, so my brother came back into the house and asked who moved his car. I was looking toward the ground as if I knew he wasn't asking me; I was too small to drive such a big car. My feet would not reach the pedal and I couldn't see over the steering wheel. My other brother confessed and we all got into a whole lot of trouble for that.

Being a kid, we often did things we had no business doing. I guess we were so intrigued with driving and wanted to see how it worked, we were willing to take a chance even if it killed us. The very next day, we tried the same thing but it did not work because my brother had unhooked the car battery. He was one step ahead of us.

Then, when I became 16, I got my learner's permit. That meant I was allowed to drive only when the sun was up but an adult must be in the car. My auntie's best friend, who was our neighbor at the time, needed me to drive her around to take care of some errands. I had just got my learner's permit, so I was excited to drive. The older woman was afraid to drive, so I drove her around. One day I was taking her to the grocery store, which was maybe 3 miles from where we lived. As I was at the traffic light, making a left hand turn, a car came out of nowhere, ran the traffic light, and smashed right into us. Although the car that ran the light was in the wrong, so tell me why I got a ticket?

The older lady who I was driving around did not tell me she had no license. That really made me angry. Here I was trying to be nice and take her around, but she never mentioned she did not have a license, so I had to pay a ticket. That was just another taste of how life can be unfair—another part of my initiation into adulthood.

Eventually I saved up enough money to buy my own car. I purchased my first car, a 1979 Buick Regal with a candy apple purple paint job, and tire rims that were in vogue. I would get up every morning, wash my car, and clean it up for the night. Once I'd finished washing it, I would park the car alongside the front yard so people passing by could see how shiny it was. Then I would stand in the house and look out the window to see how clean the car was and making sure no one touched it.

One day as I stood in the living room, looking out the window, admiring my car, I noticed one of the neighbors down the street touch my car. He knew how "anal" I was about my things, so I approached him outside and the neighbor began running. As I was running, about to tackle him, I slipped, fell, and skinned my leg. I guess God was telling me it was not good to worship material things, because I was going to beat this guy's ass for fingerprinting my car. My godsisters laughed at me because I had fallen down. I just believe in taking care of what you got and it will last a long time, but I realized I was perhaps taking this to the extreme. Imagine being so attached to a car that my whole day was occupied in making sure no one else touched it; after that incident I decided to take pride in my car and keep it in good condition and concentrate on using the car to get me places and for having good times. I began to enjoy myself a lot more after that realization.

CHAPTER **11**

Shopping Haze

I CAN REMEMBER in the mid 1970's when I thought I really "had it going on." That's when bellbottom pants were out and pointed-toe shoes were in style. I guess I wanted to be like James Brown. I heard how these shoes would make you glide across the floor. Once when my dad and I were shopping, I spotted these shoes in the window, so I asked my dad, "May I please have a pair of them?" They were only $15, so I tried the shoes on in the store. I did not want to take them off, so he bought the shoes for me. I could not wait to wear these shoes, so the following day, I wore the shoes to school with a pair of jeans. My classmates laughed at me all day long in school, calling me Elvis Presley, James Brown, etc.

Once school was out, I ran all the way home. As I reached the front door, out of breath, my dad asked, "What's wrong?" I responded, "They picked on me all day about my shoes." My dad replied, "You wanted the shoes." Cameron cried, "Dad, please take those shoes back. I don't like them anymore." Although they were so narrow they hurt my toe, I did not mention that because I thought they were cool. We tried to return the shoes, but the store would not refund the shoes; they would only issue a store credit. So now we had a track and field competition going on at school in a few days. This was my chance to get new sneakers.

When the day of track and field competition arrived, my dad refused to buy me any more shoes, so what ended up happening was that I had to wear my brother's shoes, which were 2 sizes too big. As I entered the competition, everyone was laughing at me because my shoes were too big for my feet, but I did not let that slow me down. As I started to run around the track, I could feel my feet slipping out of the shoes, which put me further back in the race, even though my brother and I were the fastest at the school. That day I lost the race, but it taught me a lot. You can't get everything you want; you get what you need and be thankful.

Years later, when I finished school, all of these credit cards and bills started coming to my house in my name. I would fill out the application, get the credit card, max it out, and then fill out another application for another card, max it out, etc., not knowing how all of these were going to affect me in the years to come.

Both parents were deceased, so there was no one to sit down with me and discuss these important things, such as opening up checking accounts, spending money out of the account, not writing checks when there is no money there to cover. I was having a good time. Now they are sending magazines to the house. I can order all kinds of things out of the magazine, just by writing a check or using my credit card. I used to go to stores, buy all kinds of jewelry, and order things for my friends. When that checking account closed, I just opened another one, not knowing how I was going to pay all this money back to whomever, because when you're young, you are not thinking clearly; all you see is buying things you like. I tell you--those were the days; when I didn't have a care in the world, as if I were invisible. But as I was eventually to find out, those were the days that got me off to a rocky start, when it seemed that working two jobs was not enough to pay off my debts incurred during youthful indiscretions.

I used to enjoy going shopping; I had a credit card and a checking account, and I felt rich. When I found out that you can rent cars with checks, it was like heaven. I used to order flowers to send to lady friends, making their day, and buying fancy outfits for the concerts. Now the sad thing was when payday rolled around, the majority of my check was gone, then later it went to the overdraft mode, and then my account was closed as I did not have enough money in my account. Then I would go to another bank, trying to beat the system. Later things got a little boring for me, so I would apply for another credit card. Being young, the banks approved these cards, and then the shopping began again.

I never knew how deeply this would affect me as I got older, spending money that I didn't really have. Lesson learned, so now I must slow my shopping and spending down.

As I got older and tried to purchase a car and apartment, I learned that my credit has a huge impact on my life for years to come. I used to use my cards to get money out to pay rent, bills, and car notes. Now I had my apartment but no furniture because I burned my credit up. The banks would not take a chance with me on credit because of the things I used to do at a young age. Then I found a bank that would give me a small limit, but that amount was not enough to furnish my place.

I was running a race called "beating the check to the bank," so that my check would not bounce. Of course it would work for the moment. Later in the month, I had several letters coming in the mail from numerous banks, demanding to make a payment by a certain date or else. I really could not afford this apartment, so I had to move out and try to pay these creditors off to keep my name and credit clear. I was panicking on how I was going to pay these people. My friends said, "You got yourself into this mess, now get out of it." But being a young kid, you don't see how much trouble you can get yourself into.

As the years passed and things were looking a lot better for me, I realized that the older you get, the more mature you become in some situations. Working two jobs and working overtime on both jobs helped me to get the bills caught up. Now it's time to purchase things with cash only. I'm on another apartment hunt, but doing everything honestly and a lot more slowly, and not trying to let my desire to please friends overpower my judgment.

Lesson learned!

But of course that was not the end of my money lessons. There are many temptations throughout life involving money –how to get it, how to report it, how to share it, how to invest it. I once applied for a job as a salesman in a clothing store, which involved being paid on a commission basis, which usually means lower earnings. The store where I would be working was located in a small mall in Miami, Florida. I worked my ass off to earn my commission; I was approaching the customers as soon as they entered the store. All the time, my manager was overseeing my earnings and the way I was communicating with the customers. My manager set up a meeting with me and asked if I would be interested in being a floor manager. I replied, "Yes, sir." So he went over a few things and trained me.

As the months passed, I felt a lot more comfortable with my work. I knew how to hire people, conduct an interview, and learned what to look for and what not to look for. So, as the year end approached, each store had a goal to reach. I was reaching my goal sure enough, but not in an honest way; I began bringing the prices down on the items without my manager's approval. So I was reaching my goal but losing merchandise at the same time. My store was audited and I was fired for those reasons. I was asked to pay all the money back that was lost. Looking back, I realize it was foolish of me to stoop to dishonesty to get ahead. It would have been better to approach my job with honesty and determination, even if it meant falling short of my goal.

CHAPTER 12

Finding Out Who I Am

IN THE EARLY 1970's I lost both parents. Getting past my parents' deaths was not an easy task. First I had to acknowledge that they were both deceased. I said to myself, "My parents would want the best for me." Then I started attending church more often, fasting and praying, opening up my mind, heart, and soul. Next I finished high school, which was a very difficult task for me, but I focused on school and working hard toward graduation. I also focused on what I would like to be doing in the years to come, so I got a little job after school.

To deal with all the anger I felt inside because of the death of my parents whom I loved so much, I used my job and school as outlets. I ran track for the school, and had a very close bond with the Lord, joining the church choir. I became more than a member in church.

I learned that if you're going to school and focus on what you have to do in school, doing your work and paying attention, you would not have so many problems in school. It is also important during those years to choose your friends wisely; try to hang around friends who want something out of life, who are already talking about what they want to be when they grow up. Nine times out of ten they are aiming for success. By praying and putting GOD first, you can avoid a lot of incidents, and He will lead you on the right path for which you are aiming.

Both during school and afterwards it's important to have a good set of values. I can remember in the 1990's, if you didn't have a car, your next step was to try to rent one. It was so easy to rent cars back then. All you needed was cash and a driver's license, and you were on your way. I did not have a car at the time, so I would rent a car every weekend. I could remember going over to friends' houses and showing off, telling them I just bought the car. I would take the stickers off the car and change the key chain to hide the name of the car rental company. So after I removed all stickers, my friends would believe it was my car. We would go riding everywhere, hanging out, and having fun. This goes to show you how much influence your friends have over you when you are willing to lie about things that aren't really important just to be cool with them. That goes to show you the things we would do for our friends' approval.

As the months went on, I got tired of renting cars and being broke at the same time, so I had to come up with a new method of getting around or change my friends. I ended up telling them the truth about the car situation. I was renting a car every week just to please them. But a real friend does not care about what you have. I stopped renting cars and started saving my money. My friends had cars, so I guess I wanted to be like them. Now my friends and I are the best and I do not have to put up a front anymore.

There are some so-called friends who would have you doing some stupid things and you would, just to maintain that friendship. It's really not that important; use your own mind and be a better judge of choosing your friends. Bringing weapons to school such as knives and guns is not cool, it's dangerous, and that's not a good friend setting you up for your future behind bars. My message to young and old is to be a leader and not a follower; that way you have the upper hand on your life.

Now that I am trying to make the right choices in life and to hang around positive people, only positive things can happen. When hanging around a group of people it takes just one bad influence to screw everything up with what would they like for you to do in order to be cool. The problem I had was trying to prove things to my friends when it really wasn't necessary.

Whether you are a child, a teenager, or an adult, you do not need a friend to justify who you are and what your capabilities are. You can make that decision on your own or with the help of a caring parent. I'm sure your parent will not guide you in the wrong direction. Kids today do not want to listen to what their mom or dad has to say about situations; why? Because in their eyes their parents are too old, they do not know what they are talking about, but at the same time, they have been down the road you are going down and at the end of that road is nothing but trouble. Kids today would rather get insight from their friends just because they are in the same age bracket, but that does not mean it's correct. By hanging around positive people with good intentions, good energy will take you in the right direction.

As teenagers in school, we were often pressured into meeting new people called classmates, not knowing anything about them, just adapting to them. It's hard to choose your friends; you don't know what their personality is like or their background. Undecided now, being a follower is not a good thing; you find yourself doing things you would not do as a leader. In my case I went through a phase of stealing from stores and checking out library books and not returning them, so when it was time to graduate, I couldn't until I paid the fines on all the books I never bothered to return. This is a good reminder that there are consequences for actions or inactions.

I can remember when I was reaching early adulthood, when I thought I had everything together, but a lady friend I was dating thought otherwise. She insisted on doing a make-over on me. The first thing to change was my haircut, which was very outdated because I was scared to try something new. Once I got my haircut, I looked like a totally different person. Next was the dress code–she selected a whole new wardrobe, fill of bright colors, different styles of pants, dress pants, ties and jeans, all name brand, of course. I was a Wrangler man and very simple, so as the makeover was completed, my self-esteem was off the chain. Now she had created a monster. Caught up in my new image, I decided I had to change my living arrangements, furniture, apartment, and transportation; all this was to meet the criteria of who I was at the time.

With these changes I became a lot more conscientious about my responsibilities. I liked the new me and knew that I could be influenced by anyone whether it's good or bad, but hoped for a good influence. You should never forget who helped you along the way. Whether it came from your moth-er, father, siblings, friends, girlfriend or boyfriend, you should never burn that bridge down; you may have to cross that bridge again. I know we sometimes feel we may not need someone anymore and start treating our spouse or partner very cruelly and rudely. We may feel we can find another person to give us a free ride; we don't have to earn their respect because we already know they love us and would do anything to keep us in their life, which is not healthy. I found myself going down that road; it took me a while, but I got back on the right track, and so can you.

There should come a time in your life when you say, "Hey, enough is enough. Wake up and smell the coffee." I'm speaking from experience. Women, you should not have to settle for anyone or anything, and men, you should want more in life. Stand up, grab your balls, and act like the man your parents dreamed of you being. My message to the readers--there is always someone for you out there. You don't have to force a relationship or settle with anyone; do not rush, take your time, and pray about it first. Pray about any decision you experience. If it's not a good one, don't make your life and your companion's life miserable; let it go and move on.

I could compare my life to a Rubik cube. I was experiencing many things in life from different angles, trying to figure out what worked for me. In life, you try to connect to certain people and to the right opportunities in order to survive. There were times I was struggling. I thought I had everything together, then later on down the line, I forgot to connect to the one and only Jesus Christ. You cannot finish your connection without involving Him in your everyday plan. I realized I have to be patient, understanding, and willing to make necessary changes. Just like a Rubik cube, you must make sure each side is aligned with the correct color in order to win.

I'm working now, moving on with my life and being independent. I have my own car, own apartment, and a pretty good job. In sum, never give up on what you believe in; be strong and stay focused on your dream.

CHAPTER 13

Music Enters My Life

A FEW MONTHS after graduating from high school, I enrolled in college, studying music. That gave me a new direction in life. My major was music, studying to pursue becoming a singer, actor, model, and dancer--all around entertainment.

While attending college, I sang in the college choir, Broadway shows, etc. It's amazing how your life can change if you choose to change and do things that inspire you. I attended the college for 1 year and some months and worked on campus in the film projector department, learning how to operate films.

Attending college courses, I met a young lady who was a classmate. We were in a couple of classes together, which brought us closer. We dated while we traveled with the college choir to the Bahamas and other events. Once we left college we were still dating for a while, and she inspired me to stay in the entertainment field. Yes, being in the entertainment field, we were constantly busy, which caused our relationship to go sour, but we have stayed in contact. She's doing great and married. We are getting older and understand things a lot better, starting with the importance of life.

I can remember coming home from school one day, while going to class and working on campus in the aviation department. I was working later than usual. I believe the bus stopped running at a certain time. I was living in Carol City, a city near Miami, Florida, with the pastor of my church.

I had no other way home. While walking down the street, looking for the nearest phone booth to make a call to my pastor's husband to pick me up from school, a white car slowed down. As my heart was pounding, a Caucasian gentleman asked, "Do you need a ride?" I replied, "No, thank you," and proceeded to walk. So he pulled off and I moved further down the street, trying to make it to a phone booth. We did not have cell phones then.

The man made a U-turn, slowed down again, and asked, "Are you sure you don't need a ride?" I replied, "No, sir." As I began to pick up my pace, the car began to speed up behind me, so I ran into a night club, asking for help, but it was a club full of Caucasians. I stayed in the club until the guy left, not knowing he was parked outside on the opposite side of the club. I began running. I made the phone call to my pastor's husband; he was on his way to pick me up. Now as I was waiting, the club was closing also.

I started running behind the school campus, trying to hide from this guy. As I was running in the dark behind the school campus, I didn't know there was a lake behind the campus. I was running so fast, I almost jumped into the lake. This guy was still chasing me. While my heart was pounding faster, the guy got out of his car to chase me. Finally, I ran back in front of the college campus where there were lights and people driving up and down the streets.

Now I saw the pastor's husband's van coming down the street. I felt so relieved and tired. Raymond asked, "What is going on? Why are you breathing so hard?" I told him,

"Someone was chasing me." When Raymond pulled up, I pointed out the car and the guy sped off. He wanted to find the guy, but I said, "No." I was just happy to see Raymond coming.

So the very next day, I told my employer I could not work for him anymore because the bus stopped running at a certain time. I explained to my supervisor what happened and why I could not work. He said that since I'm a good worker and was attending college here, he would change my shift to early release. I thanked GOD for His being there when I needed Him. The moral of that story is to pay close attention to your surrounding areas; it could very well happen to you.

Living with the pastor helped me out a great deal. There were days I would go to work with the pastor's husband and kids, doing lawn service every weekend. There were times I did not want to work with them, so I would hide under the bed until they were gone. Every Saturday Raymond would wake us up at 6 a.m. to cut grass in the neighbors' yards. We would get paid maybe $50 a week; I was trying to make enough money to move out on my own and I refused to go cut yards; I knew I needed to make a lot more than that.

However, I continued attending church and getting closer to my Maker. I really do love the relationship I have with the Lord, going to Bible study, understanding the Bible and the messages in the Word. It helped me to get through a lot of things.

I prayed every day, hoping I could find a job making my own money and getting my own apartment. One day I learned that if you really want something bad enough, you have to go after it. Years passed; I landed a job at an elementary school as a security guard, which helped me make money and handle some things that needed special attention. I worked there for

8 years; it helped me make ends meet until I found another way to make extra money.

A friend of my brother's godmother was holding auditions for male exotic dancers. The auditioning was being held at a night club in Liberty City, Florida. While the auditioning was going on, I waited to hear from them.

I also teamed up with a young lady by the name of Cindy. Cindy and I were both inspired by music, so we decide to form a duet; the name we chose was the New Generation, but Cindy called me by the nickname Baldee. As duet singers, we would practice every weekend at Betty's house. Betty was my brother Randall's godmother, and she allowed us to rehearse at her home.

Then she became our manager. Betty would book clubs and locate talent shows. We would perform at talent shows and often would win. We also performed in night clubs for thousands of dollars in cash and prizes.

Cindy and I sang together for 7 years. Later I started performing solo, so Cindy and I decided to go our separate ways while I tried a solo career. We would occasionally rejoin one another and enter contests once again and sing at weddings.

As the years passed, I heard Cindy was getting sick and was not feeling too well, so she stopped singing and started focusing on her health. She was a wonderful singer. Later a tragedy occurred--she passed away. My heart was so sad. Her last words to me were, "Baldee, keep singing. You have a great voice." Rest in peace, Cindy.

Later I heard good news from the leader of the group for which I auditioned to be a male dancer. I passed the audition, and began to perform in night clubs, making pretty good money, performing 3 nights a week.

The pay was not that much at first, until you built up your clients. However, the tips were awesome. I would also perform at private parties, making good money. There were times we would be out performing all night doing double performances; the business was what you made of it.

So now the clubs were having dance contests, best dressed, and singing contests. I would enter each and every one to help build up my fan base. I was very successful; I assumed I built up a fan base because each time I would enter a contest, I would win. Now I guessed I was so good, I would enter the contest against the NFL football players. The manager of the group which is over me entered me in the male exotic dancer contest, as small as I was. I would compete against these huge NFL players; with the skills and technique I had, I would win 1st place each and every time.

This club also had a singing competition, so I entered the talent show. I felt a little nervous. I was so used to Cindy performing with me, so I prayed to Cindy and asked her to meet me in spirit at this club, so that I could enter this contest without fear. I felt her presence; I could hear her voice saying, "Sing like never before. You got this." I went up on stage; I was a little nervous because there were some very talented people there. My performance was awesome. As the contest was taking place, I could not believe how much support I had; it was a great turnout. I won the contest--cash money and a trophy.

The club would have contests every week. I would go there every weekend and win the contest. They would also have a female and male best dressed contest, where you would model the attire that you were wearing,

I was in the entertainment field for 17 years or so. As the years went by, I would perform only at big events. I would model at fashion shows. For a few years, I would try a little of everything. The dancing slowed down and I was not working a steady job at the time. I decided now was the time to try my fortune somewhere else.

CHAPTER **14**

Peachy in Georgia

LATER I MOVED away to Cordele, Georgia with Betty's mother. She was someone my father had dated years ago before he passed away. I always stayed in touch with her; she's a wonderful person. Betty's mother's name was Leola; she had that caring, loving mother's intuition.

So I was living in Cordele, Georgia with Leola. It was pretty different there. Cordele, Georgia is a lot slower and things were different there after coming from a big place like Miami, Florida.

As the days went by, I decided to start looking for a job there. The atmosphere felt pretty friendly, and the people made you feel welcome. The job market there might have been a lot more welcoming.

My job search was a little challenging. If I landed a job; it may not have been the job I was searching for, but I started working one week after my arrival there. I worked in the field picking pecans; that's something I'd never done. It was pretty hot out there working in the field. The job involved picking pecans off the ground and putting them in a Croker sack. You would get paid by the weight of the bags. Sometimes I would find an acorn which I would put between the pecans in order to maximize the weight.

I thought I would work out there in the field for a while until I landed another job. Yes, I searched for another job, but since I was working there, I thought I might as well make the best of this job. That's what I told a few of my friends whom I met living in Georgia.

Since Leola knew a few people who had their own businesses, I asked her to speak to someone who would help me find a job. As the weeks went by, I was still in search of another job. Through my job search, I tried to adjust to the city as well. Leola really made me feel like family. She helped me when needed: she would speak with some of the people who she knew to help me to get a job, although it was tough there at the time. Leola did not pressure me into getting a job just yet. Months later, I was still searching for a job with no luck. So my godsisters and brothers and I would sit on the front porch, just chilling with our friends, day after day with nothing to do but hang out with friends and walk the streets.

Months later, as we were all sitting on the front porch talking, Leola came outside and shouted, "Y'all need to get your asses up and look for a job. No job is going to come to you!!" We laughed while sitting on the porch. Ten minutes later, a guy came out of nowhere and asked, "Does anyone want to work?" We called Leola and once she came out on the porch, we told her, "We have a job. This guy just stopped by and asked if anyone wanted a job."

So we all were hired to work at the farmers market, Monday through Friday. The job was not easy and it was hot every day loading and unloading watermelons, loading them neatly on a truck for them to sell by the truckload.

The job was okay, but who wants to be throwing watermelons? That was too much like working. I was still on a job search. I had a friend who worked at the supermarket around the corner from our house. One day I had lunch with my friend to see if he would speak to his manager about my being employed there. I landed a job there which was great; things started to move for me.

I worked at the supermarket in the deli department. Servicing our customers was a great experience and the manager was pleased with how quickly I learned the store. After I had been working there a few months, he asked me what I thought about being promoted as an assistant manager. I answered, "Yes sir, I would love to."

While I was working at the store, I still searched for a better paying job and eventually located a school for mechanics that offered pay while attending school. So I decided to give it a try, and attended school while working at the store. I was eager to learn yet another skill to help me find a decent paying job, and I thanked God things were slowly looking up for me.

In school, I felt a lot better. Once I was off work at the market, my friends would stop by and we would all go to the skating rink, which was the only excitement on Sunday night. So years passed, I received my certificate in mechanics, and the store was closing about the same time I was completing my course. Thus seemed to be a signal to me to leave the peachy, pecan State of Georgia.

CHAPTER 15

Fun in Florida

ONE YEAR AFTER leaving Florida, I decided to move back to Miami, Florida. Soon I was back on a job search again, living from house to house, trying to get myself together. I landed a job as a paraprofessional at a middle school, working with special needs kids and normal kids in the 6th grade. After I passed the audition as a male dancer, I would work some nights and weekends; doors began to open for me.

The special needs kids had all kinds of disabilities, mental and physical. I feel that was the best job ever, as I was in these kids' lives for years. I helped give these kids hope and smiles. I would treat these students as normal kids, letting them know that they could do anything if they put their mind to it. As the years passed, I was invited to a couple of their graduations. The parents invited me at their child's request; I guess I made a difference in these kids' lives. Today these kids are adults, and they keep in touch with me. They thank me for taking the time to help them realize their potential. This experience made me realize that having special needs does not mean you can't do better or accomplish things you desire to do.

As the years passed, I made another move and that was to

Oxford, Mississippi with friends, just trying something new. I lived there for one month, got homesick and running out of money, so I would dance up there in clubs, which does not pay as well as Florida. Moving there was the worst mistake ever, but I was still learning about life. It was cold there. The heat in my car went out, so I would ride around with a blanket in my car to stay warm. It's funny now, but back then it was not.

As the months passed, it was getting colder and the people whom I was living with really wanted money.

My money was low; I was stuck up there miles and miles away from my family. I did not want to bother my family about money, so I made a phone call to one of my homies, Brandon, who helped me out with the situation. I asked for a certain amount and within 15 minutes, money was at Western Union, waiting for me.

So I began to pack up my car and got an oil change. The very next day, I started driving back to Miami. During that time, according to the news, a severe hurricane called Andrew was in progress. That storm destroyed a lot of areas down there. As I was driving back to Miami, all I could think about was my family, knowing they were in the area where the storm hit. The apartment where my sister was living was hit as well, so now I was worried.

As I got closer to Miami, I saw trees down, light poles down all across the street, and traffic lights down, so I immediately started driving to Homestead to my sister's place. I saw all kinds of debris in the streets. As I got closer to my sister's place, my heart began to drop. No one was there, so I drove around looking for her. As I continued to drive around, I saw people standing on top of their cars, yelling and screaming.

Suddenly, there they were–my sister and her family. My heart was very happy and they were glad to see me; I was more than happy to see them. I picked them up and brought them to my brother's house in Fort Lauderdale, Florida.

In the weeks that followed, I continued to perform as a dancer until another job came through for me. Then one day I ran into an old friend who worked at a law firm as a CPA. His manager asked if he knew someone who would like to work for their firm, so he located me and asked if I would like to work there. I prayed to the Lord that something would come through for me, and He did bless me with a great long-term job. I have worked for this CPA law firm for years. They are the best people you could ever work for; just like a family. Years later I joined another CPA law firm, which was much larger than the original firm. I learned a lot of different jobs, enhancing skills that I was not aware of.

While at the law firm I absorbed a lot of information on how to handle problems. This knowledge led me to do a favor for one of my friends. She was having problems at home with her husband, so she wanted to hire a private investigator to follow him around to see why he was not coming home. I told her I could do that for her, so I began my private investigator work. I located this guy in several spots, restaurants and stores and at a young lady's house. I went to this lady's house as if I were selling cookies, so as I went to ring the doorbell, he came to the door and I made my sale. I asked, "Is your wife home?" He replied, "No, she's not my wife, she's my girl-friend" (immediately busted).

So I shared that information with my friend so she could see for herself what she was up against. Years passed; my client got a divorce. Once she came back to work, she looked like a brand new person. Of course she offered to pay me, but

I did not accept it; she was a nice person who did not deserve what she got. It goes to show you--someone is always watching whether you know it or not. And money cannot buy you happiness--that's something that has to be earned.

Being an entertainer at night and working a day job kept me busy. I used to travel to different states performing as a male dancer. The money was good for me and a couple of my dancing partners would travel to different colleges, performing there for the women at their parties, but we did experience a lot of ups and downs in the business.

In the entertainment field, I would go to a lot of casting calls for movies and sitcom TV series; to name a few, The Sopranos, White Christmas, Kelsey Grammar, Out of Time, and Denzel Washington. I'm still working as an extra on some TV series. Times were pretty rough back then, so I did whatever it took to make extra money to pay bills. In the entertainment field, you meet people. After years in the business, I had a son; it was not planned but things do happen. You have to be responsible for your actions, so I had to work harder than ever, working (2) jobs in entertainment and working at a CPA law firm.

I quit my job as a school security guard and worked as a male exotic dancer to help ends meet and it worked for a while. While in the entertainment field, you have to treat your fans nice whether they are big, small, unattractive, etc., but they all have feelings and money. I performed at various night clubs; that's how you build your fan base. You have to cater to all types and sizes of women.

There were days these women would have certain areas sectioned off in the club. They would have the big girls section, then the petite girls section, and so on. I learned that the healthy girls pay plenty of money. As I was performing for them, one of the heavier women came out on the dance floor. I must say she weighed about 300 pounds and I weighed about 170. She landed on top of me and I heard my knee snap. After I heard that, I knew I could not move. I had to crawl off stage--I was down for the count. Ever since then, my knee was never the same, but all these incidents come with the territory and you just have to be ready for the unexpected.

The entertainment business can be a dirty business. There are times I would have people stalking me just because I was in the limelight, but you really can make money in the business, if you have the right clients who are willing to pay. You would have your good fans as well as your enemies, just because you are in the business. There would be times I was performing and all of a sudden, a bottle would come flying at me. The reason would be that one of my fan's boyfriend or husband was upset because their wife or significant other was enjoying what she saw. I experienced shootings in the clubs while performing, tables being thrown, and fights taking place. So for those of you who ever thought about being a dancer, think twice. There are times you would be at the club at 12 midnight, but would not perform till 3 a.m.; it's the business. Through it all and both jobs, I saved up enough money to get my own apartment. That was a big step for me in maintaining responsibility for my child.

I learned that when you're looking for an apartment, it pays to take your time. And the key to apartment hunting, try to drive by the apartment complex at night. That will tell the truth about what kind of place you're getting into. Or go to an agency; they usually can give you the "ok" whether it's a safe development or not. Sometime things look good on the outside but are not always good on the inside. Now I have a good job, I found an apartment which was not too far from my job in a very quiet neighborhood, and not too many kids hanging around outside. I was all moved in, my neighbors were older people and a young couple on the other side of me.

Once when I came home from work around midnight, as I opened my door, I saw things thrown around in my apartment. I saw a lot of my items were missing; I was very upset. I was devastated; after working so hard to have my place just like I wanted, it was all gone. So I called 911, made a police report, and filed an insurance claim. Thankfully, I had renter's insurance, even though I thought I didn't have to worry about theft, as the neighborhood seemed safe. Thank God everything was covered under the insurance.

I was left feeling my privacy had been violated. How could I remain living there? The very next day, I spoke with the leasing office and asked if I could be moved, knowing I couldn't live there once my place was invaded. A month later, they moved me to a different unit. In the new unit, I purchased rental insurance and an alarm, just to feel a little secure.

I was planning to take a trip out of town with my dancing partners; we had a show in Virginia. The next day, I can remember driving to Virginia state, which I had never been to before. As we approached our destination, it was very cold. I was looking around at snow everywhere. As we stopped for gas, we prepared to make a pit stop, and the driver got in touch with friends nearby. As I was getting out of the car, we noticed a guy was on the steps, sleeping in the cold. As we got closer, we realized he was not sleeping, he was dead on the steps; I assumed he froze to death. I thought you would only see these things on TV. I wondered how often that happens up there, but it goes to show you how blessed you are and to appreciate what you have.

I learned a valuable lesson from that experience. There are so many homeless people on the streets, and you never know what they are going through that drove them to be where they are. When you see people on the streets like that, give them a few dollars. That person in need could be Jesus and you turn your back on them. One day that could be you or a sibling of yours.

So we finally reached our destination at the center, where we performed, which was a good night, although it was cold. The fans came out to support us. On our way back home, we stopped and bought food and fed a couple of homeless people. It felt so good to do a good deed. We also gave out a couple of dollars to some homeless. Every little bit helped. It was a successful trip.

On my way back home, I was still a little puzzled about living in that area of Miami. I could not rest; I noticed there were all kinds of young people moving and hanging out at all times of night. So I embarked on an apartment hunt again, looking for something a little quieter, in a gated area. But I thought of something while I was searching--sometimes the company you keep can make your neighbors think differently of you. As the saying goes, "it's not where you live, it's how you live." So I moved when I found something gated with fewer apartment units in the North Miami area of Florida. My neighbors are elderly people.

So I moved into my new neighborhood, put everything together in my new place, and felt a lot better, with a brand new start. Living next door to me was an elderly woman. At first I didn't realize that she lived alone. Her kids were around my age, and they would come see her maybe twice a month, which was not enough of a visit for an elderly person.

They were paying her rent and monthly expenses. I really felt bad for her. There were days I would come home from work, and she would be walking the streets, so I would slow my car down and ask her, "How come you are so far from home?" She would reply, "I'm going to the store for some ice cream." I felt so bad because the store really was too far for her to walk, about 8 blocks from where we lived, so I asked her to get in the car and offered to take her back home. Not knowing she was leaving her front door open, I would drop her off at her home, go back to the store, get her a pint of ice cream, and bring it to her home. So I told her from now on, I'd buy her a pint of ice cream twice a week, which brought a smile to her face. From then on, I would make it my job to go next door to check on her every other day, and as I went to the door, I'd ask if there was anything else she might need.

On weekends, I would do a serious cleaning in my apartment. I would leave my door open, sweeping and dusting. I had plants that needed dusting and watering. While I was vacuuming my carpet, I would see my neighbor passing by, look into my apartment, and compliment me on my flowers. Then I would ask her to come in, and I would serve her a bowl of ice cream to enjoy while I was cleaning my place. We would sit down and talk, and she would tell me her kids did not visit her often enough.

This experience with my elderly neighbor goes to show that you should treat people the way you want to be treated. They do not have to be a sibling or parents; we all are family in GOD'S eyes. You never know when someone may have to help you or watch over you as you get older, or in any situation you may not be able to handle.

When I first moved into my new apartment, I thought it was a safe community. One morning, though, as I was going to my car to go to work, I could not find my car. Someone had stolen my car! I was shocked. I walked around the whole complex looking for it. I made a police report, as my car had nice wheels on it, which I believed would attract thieves. The police officer located my car on a block with the wheels gone, just when I thought everything was safe there.

My lease was up for renewal, so I decided to move again, but I felt bad about moving. I did not want to leave my elderly neighbor--I felt it was my responsibility to watch over her. That morning I had packed and loaded up the truck to move out, when I saw my neighbor standing in the hall. She approached me and asked if I was going to the store. I replied, "I'm moving out." My heart dropped. I bought her a couple of pints of ice cream and she sat there with tears in her eyes. I was a little teary myself and I said to myself, "Who's going to look after her?" I told her I would make it my business to stop by and visit her 3 times a month. She smiled and I began to walk to my car, as she waved goodbye to me. That was the worst feeling I ever experienced. Before I moved out, I ask the landlord to please keep an eye on my ex-neighbor for me. I explained to him that her kids seldom came to visit her, so she was by herself in that unit, and I was a little concerned that she was too old to be living alone, so he promised to check in on her.

Months went by. I moved and was settled in my new place. I went by to visit my elderly friend as I had promised her I would do. Once when I knocked on her apartment door, there was no answer, so I went to the leasing office and asked the landlord what happened to the lady who was in Apartment 223. He replied, "She died 2 weeks ago." Oh, my heart dropped. I could not believe it! Such a painful feeling came over me, as if she were a family member. I said to him,

"What happened? She was okay 2 weeks ago prior to my moving." I felt bad for a couple of days; I asked if he had any information on her, such as the funeral arrangements. He had no information, so I replied, "I would like to leave a card and flowers for the family just in case you hear from her kids." I put my contact information on the card, but months passed by, and I never heard from anyone. I take comfort in the fact that we shared many happy moments over ice cream!

CHAPTER 16

Georgia on My Mind Again

MY SISTER AND I were thinking about moving and we discussed moving to Atlanta, Georgia. There are better opportunities there, the pay rate there is higher and the cost of living there is not too expensive. I hear the atmosphere is a lot more welcoming. You also get to see the seasons change. I've never experienced that, nor have I seen snow in Miami. In Miami, you only have one season—that's summer year round, other than the hurricane season. That's not something people like to experience at all.

I heard that it gets so cold sometimes in Atlanta, where you would experience icicles at times. I also heard that the atmosphere is a lot friendlier. Martin Luther King, Jr. lived there and had gone through so much there, and there are many memories of him there. There are some historical places there, including the church he attended. I was planning a trip there, so I could visit and see what it's like before we moved my sister and her family there. I knew it would be a lot more cosmopolitan than my visit to Cordele years earlier, and I was excited at the opportunities that awaited me.

It was going to be a big change for me. I heard that if you

wanted to pursue your career for whatever it is, this is the place for it: singer, model, actor, entertainer. I heard there are a lot of connections there. I would just have to take it seriously if that's what I wanted to do. I knew that I had gone through hard times and didn't know what I wanted to do with myself, but being away from home in a brand new state, trying out new experiences, I would have to buckle down. I had a couple of interviews set up for when I made the visit. While filling out applications online, I was getting plenty of responses for job interviews the very next day, but I had to inform them I was in Miami and would be there visiting soon, so I might interview then. As I was submitting plenty of applications, the replies were coming faster than I expected, and I was feeling very optimistic about my prospects in Georgia.

One day while I was at work, a co-worker asked me if I really wanted to move. I replied, "Of course." I told her my sister was thinking about moving there with me, and I didn't want her to move alone, so I would join her. I told my sister, "It sounds good, but it's going to be a big change for the both of us and your kids." So I asked my job for that time off to make an exploratory trip, and they granted me the time off, but I did not speak about my future plans, as I was not sure of what my plans were. As the months passed and the days were narrowing down, I was getting excited and a little nervous at the same time. What if I went and didn't like it after making a move and leaving my job behind?

During my visit to Atlanta, I was in charge of looking for an apartment. I located a certain area on the outskirts of Atlanta, so when we decided to move, at least we would have some idea of neighborhoods to visit. We decided to go ahead with the move, so we planned a second trip to select an apartment, sign a lease, and put a deposit down. Once we were approved and had the utilities set up, we were ready to make the move.

Next I spoke to my manager and gave my job two weeks' notice. They were sad about it but were happy for me at the same time. Once I started packing, the doubts returned and a host of "what ifs" occurred to me--my nerves were getting the best of me. My manager said to me, "If things do not work out there, you can always come back to your job." I felt a lot more at ease then. On my last day at the job, they gave me a going-away party and a bonus, just in case I needed anything. I had been with that law firm for 15 years. I knew I was really going to miss them; we were all like family, but I looked forward to a new beginning for my sister and her family and me.

So we finished packing and getting ready to get on the long road to Atlanta, Georgia. I drove a 24-foot truck on the highway. The trip was about 600 miles long and involved driving 10 hours non-stop. I was excited but sleepy at the same time. My sister was driving behind me in her truck. We did not do too much stopping except for gassing up, which was expensive. We were trying to make this trip as short as possible. After awhile I started getting sleepy, swerving on the road. My sister noticed it from behind, so I pulled over and let my brother drive for a few minutes. I tried to rest while my brother was driving. After he drove for 30 minutes, he was swerving as well, so we pulled into a gas station where I pur- chased a Snickers candy bar and a Coke. These refreshments kept me awake all the way to our destination. We finally ar- rived in Atlanta, Georgia at 9:00 a.m.

We were all tired, drained, and hungry. The apartment leasing office did not open until 10:00 a.m., so we stopped and had breakfast at a restaurant in the plaza located down the street from the apartment, which was the worst food ever. $60 down the drain on awful food!

After that terrible breakfast, we returned to the apartment to unload the truck. It was a nice apartment, but the unit was all the way in the back of the woods. We did not like where that unit was located. We spoke with the assistant manager and informed him we had just moved there and we would like a nicer unit. Since we were paying our rent in advance for a year, he relocated us to a nice unit in the front of the complex, which was a lot better. Paying rent for a whole year gave us plenty of time to locate a job, so I would search for a job for a whole week, and then wait the following week for phone calls.

My first call back from my job search was from a well known department store, Wal-Mart. They were hiring cashiers, so I submitted an application; I never thought I would be working for this big company. Having just moved to Atlanta, I appreciated any kind of job at this time. As I had always worked office jobs, this was totally different, but I enjoyed it. I was a cashier who needed plenty of training. It was great working with people hand-in-hand until I got this job "down pat." I became one of the best and fastest cashiers ever.

Working a cash register, you must be people-oriented and learn how to greet your customer in a timely manner with a smile, ring up the sale, and bag groceries at the same time. As the weeks passed, I became more familiar with the system. I had customers now coming in asking for me, and they would prefer coming in my line because I moved them in and out so rapidly. Customers went to my manager, giving me good recommendations and great feedback from their experience with me as a cashier.

The job was going so well, I did not realize I would be working there for 3 years; time flies by when you enjoy what you're doing. I never gave up my search for another job; in fact I'm still applying for jobs to see what opportunities arise. I received a raise about 1 month after working there, which was pretty good. I learned to work different departments, such as electronics, shoes, and layaway departments. I also worked in the toy department. I was willing to learn as much as I could just in case I wanted to grow in the company. I also decided to go to a temporary agency and apply for other jobs, either full-time or part-time.

I went to a temporary agency searching for another job and a short time later I was invited to apply for a full-time job, working for the lottery in the mailroom. After submitting my application, the Georgia lottery asked me to come in for an interview. The interview went well; my job duties were to deliver mail to certain areas within the huge plant where they print the tickets. However, lottery employees were not allowed to play the lottery.

Delivering the mail was a pretty easy job. I noticed they had an opening for an assistant, which required data entry and drawing the tickets from the barrel for the second chance drawing, working with the manager of the lottery. I applied for and obtained that position, which paid a lot more money. I would be blindfolded and pull 200 tickets or more, where some people would win money and prizes. It was a great job and helped me to maintain my bills. I worked there for a while until I was terminated, proud of the fact that by working smart and hard, I was able to advance. However, there were still no guarantees that the good times would last forever.

Once again I went on a job search. I had resigned from Wal-Mart as a cashier once I was hired at the lottery. Have you ever gone on a job search and were rejected for no reason at all, even though you fit the criteria which they were searching for? I filled out the application for a job for which I had 16 years' experience in the field of acounting. Two days passed and no answer. One week passed by, so finally I gave them a call and they set up an interview.

After my interview, I assumed they liked my responses, as they had called me in for a second interview with 3 managers on a conference call. So I said to myself, "They like me." Everything was going great, and according to my resumé and interview, I had this job. I discussed different types of forms with them, what each form meant, and what they were used for. I was telling them of things that they had no knowledge of, but would be beneficial to the firm. They appreciated that, so they set up a third interview with the supervisors who were in charge of that department.

The managers were amazed by all the forms and documents we discussed. I gave them all kinds of ideas and knowledge of certain things, so after that interview went great, I knew I'd be starting soon. However, two days went by and finally, I received a call on the third day. The only answer they had was that they were going to hire from within.

I felt so rejected for no reason, and I must say, I really believed in my heart that the supervisors thought if they hired me their jobs were in jeopardy, as I knew a lot more than what they were trained on. Although I did not get the job, I felt a lot better once I received a phone call from a young woman saying, "Your interviews went great." She didn't understand why I was not selected, but she felt the same way I did--the supervisors had a lot to do with it, but I never gave up.

I continued my job search until someone gave me a chance. I submitted applications all over. Finally I received a phone call from Publix, which is a good company to work for, asking me to come in for an interview. They had a job opening for a stock guy, which was something I had never done--working the a.m. shift, stocking shelves, unloading trucks. So I said, "Sure, I will be there." I felt it would be a great workout for me.

My work hours were 7:00 p.m. – 3:00 a.m. I enjoyed working for Publix. I see why every time I used to shop there, the products on the shelves were so nice and neat, due to the overnight stock crew. Now I feel better, being a part of that clean store. I worked there for several months, and was still on a job search; I needed something in the morning, so that I might keep working at Publix during the night shift.

At the same time, my sister was thinking about moving back to Miami, Florida, so I had to prepare myself for being up here without her. My sister found it challenging to adjust to a different state, where there is winter, spring, summer, and fall after living in Florida where it is summer year round. She wanted to be closer to our older sister who was staying in an assisted living facility in Miami, as well. She needed someone to check on her every other week to make sure all her needs were being taken care of.

So my sister moved back to Miami, and I had to choose between staying alone in Atlanta or moving back to Miami. At the same time, I was in search of a second job to provide me with more money. Before my sister moved back to Miami, I wanted to have a physical exam, so I would know what my health care needs were while she was in Atlanta. Years earlier I was planning to have my physical done, but I backed out of it. You know, we men never like going to the doctor or maintaining our health.

Finally I made an appointment for my physical exam, and nervously waited for my results. A week later, my results came in and my doctor made an appointment for me to come back.

Everything was good with the exception of my blood pressure, which was a little higher than normal. That was good news, so I began taking control of my pressure. Although he put me on pills to help me lower it, I also needed to exercise, eat right, lay off the fried food, and do 40 minutes of cardio every day. So now I'm in control of my blood pressure. This told me that it's never too late to change your lifestyle, replacing bad habits with good ones.

So I told my sister the results. Then she could leave Atlanta and go back to Miami, knowing her baby brother was okay.

So I went back to my job search, knowing that my physical condition was good. I spoke with an old friend of mine from Miami, who had been living in Atlanta for years. I told him I was working for Publix, but needed a job making pretty good money, so I could maintain my apartment and transportation. So he spoke to a friend of his and they asked for my resumé--he would try to speak to friends to see who was hiring. Days went by before I heard from anyone. I began to pray and asked the Lord to please send me something. Finally my patience paid off. My friend asked me to drop my resumé off to a friend at an insurance company, and later the supervisor phoned me to come in for an interview.

The interview went well; two days later they called and asked if I could come in to work. I replied, "Most certainly." Thank you, God, for the job and the connection. So I went to work for an insurance company in the mailroom; I had good benefits, great hours, pretty good money, and very friendly co-workers. My job search still continued. The same day I started working for the insurance company, I landed another interview working at the GA 400 toll; two weeks later, I was hired at the toll also. I prayed and thanked the Lord for giving me two jobs, one for the week days and one on the weekend.

I thanked the good Lord for the jobs because I was paying child support with one job and the other job helped with my bills as the years passed living in Atlanta. Moving from apartment to apartment, I was not making the money that I am now. The government was taking the majority of my paycheck from one job and bills were piling up. Sometimes I felt like I was just working to pay bills, with no time to enjoy it.

The most distressing phone call I received was from Child Support saying I had $25,000 dollars backlog to pay for child support. I almost passed out--my pressure was so high, I felt warm all over, but I bit the bullet and and started making payments to take care of that issue. Years went by and by and by. Finally I finished paying the child support thanks to my God and the jobs and my tax returns. That was the best feeling ever.

Another time, after I lost my job in a department store for making a stupid mistake, I prayed and ask the Lord to please give me another chance, so he did. I received a phone call from the law firm I had left years before to move to Atlanta. They asked me to please come back, and offered me higher pay as well. I was told they could never keep anyone there at that job. They hired several people to fill my position, but they were not as humble and quick to learn preparing tax returns. I was honored to work for them again; we were one big family.

Now I could save money and try to live like normal people. I thought about buying a brand new car and I did. It goes to show you readers--you can do anything you want if you put God first and your best effort forward. That is why I can say thank you, GOD. Through everything I've experienced, good and bad, with the death of both my parents, and the struggles, witnessing my father being murdered at the age of 8 in front of my eyes, the abusive up-bringing living with my Aunt Regina, and the death of my siblings really took a toll on me. So did dealing with the things my handicapped sister had to endure. And I moved from place to place, screwing up my credit. My life was never easy--every day was a struggle. I could never purchase a new car due to the status of my credit. I really had to grow up fast so that I could catch up on life.

I thank God for giving me a second chance to make everything right with my life. Now my credit is a lot better. I purchased a new 2013 car. I can save money in the bank. I have a better job that I love because I can be trained in different departments. My child support is paid off. A few co-workers at my job ask how come I'm happy every day at work. If it was not for the Lord on my side, tell me, where would I be? He was there all the time--these are the reasons I smile every day. Once you finish reading my book, you will understand why I can smile. I've had enough heartache. I have no more room to cry. It's time to thank GOD for having my back through it all. Amen. Amen.

CHAPTER 17

Words of Encouragement

DEAR READERS, FROM all my experiences, which I certainly did not expect or desire, I have learned that it is possible to live through and learn from them, and eventually triumph. So from all my years of sorrow, struggle, and peace, I would like to extract the wisdom of my experiences:

1. Always put your precious children first. Be responsible for providing their basic needs (food, shelter, clothing, health care, and schooling), but beyond that it is important to spend quality time with them. Change his Pampers, feed him, hold him and hug him, take him to school and doctor's appointments, play with him, read books to him, share special activities such as feeding the birds, gazing at stars, going fishing or drag racing, teaching him to ride a bike.

    As your child grows up, be an example to your child, hoping he or she will follow your footsteps, as we deal with a lot of things going on in their world tomorrow.

    The world has changed; today's world has technology not known a generation ago: the internet, video games, iPhones, iPads. There is also an unprecedented wave of robbing, stealing, killing, and drugs. At the end of the day, you have choices in life: what you want to be, what you would like to do in life. The company you keep and your surroundings have a lot to do with the judgment you exercise.

2. Try your best to work out any conflicts with your spouse to avoid divorce, but if separation is necessary to end constant fighting, then please let your children know they are loved and will be taken care of.

Between responsible parents, it should not be necessary to go to court to get a child support order; the parent who is not living with the child full time should work out a reasonable amount of support and send the check to the parent and keep records of these amounts to avoid future disputes.

We should never let the government raise our kids, order us to take care of our parental responsibilities, and tell us how much to spend on our kids. We should never let them tell us when to visit our children or for how long. Reasonable parents can work out these details for themselves.

3. You may never know when is the last time you will see people who are important to you, so express your feelings and thoughts of love while they are here on earth.

4. Begin to start dreaming big and focusing on the right thing to do in life early in life to make your dreams come true. Prayer can change things and it can change you; it's never too late. Don't let time pass you by while you give up hope.

5. Kids, love where you are today and tomorrow, and appreciate who you are and who your parents are and embrace it. Parents, instill in your kids what's right and what's wrong. Kids, learn how to maintain your trustworthiness, knowing how important it is to you. It may not mean anything to you now, but trust me, it's going to follow you all the days of your life that you are here on earth.

    I find myself thinking a lot about my parents. I share with them everything that's happened to me since they left this earth. I thank them for bringing me to life and for giving me the love and caring that has sustained me in the years of my life.

    If my parents were alive today, I know I would be helping them if they needed any kind of assistance. I would shower them with that same love they showed me in the short time they were here in my life. I would continue to massage my mother's legs with lotion. We would continue talking about the good and bad things, celebrating Mother's Day, introduce her to her grandson, attend church; we would do the things that loving parents do. Please, never take your parents for granted. One day they may no longer be in your life.

6. Don't try too hard to please your friends. a real friend will be there for you no matter what you are going through. Don't get caught up in false values. Be a leader, not a follower. You can do everything you choose to do. Just put your mind, heart, and soul to it. If you surround yourself with positive, honest people, nothing but positive should come out.

7. Don't do foolish things that will wreck your credit. Instead, build credit by making a responsible purchase and make your payments in time. Don't spend beyond your means. You cannot get anything with bad credit; it only makes things harder and it makes the creditors very cautious about giving you credit because of your past history.

8. Do not give up. Pray and believe that everything is going to be all right, if you just pray and believe. The Lord is always on your side. He wants you to change your life if you've taken a wrong path and will help you on the right path if you work with Him.

9. Keep God first in any and everything you do. Keeping Him first will make everything go a lot smoother and you will make better decisions in life. Pray before that job search or interview. Enjoy each and every day and minute, month, and year the Lord grants you here on earth. Forgive the people who did you wrong and pray for them. Then pray for yourself. I have a close bond with my God. I thank him each and every day of my life, from the top of my head to the bottom of my feet for everything.

CPSIA information can be obtained
at www.ICGtesting.com
Printed in the USA
BVHW040823150620
581303BV00009B/186

9 781478 780519